Nursing
PHARMACOLOGY
- Study Notebook -

Hello Nurse

Your Feedback is Appreciated!!!

Please consider leaving us "5 Stars" on your
Amazon review.

Thank you!

This Nursing Pharmacology Study Book
Belongs To:

Mary Kaczynski

Address: 17433 Starlite Drive, south Bend, IN 46614

Phone Number: (574) 222-3447

E-mail: mkaczynski01@saintmarys.edu

Pharmacology

GENERIC NAME

BRAND NAME

DRUG CLASS

ROUTE

HIGH ALERT

☐ YES   ☐ NO

THERAPEUTIC USES

MECHANISMS OF ACTION

ADVERSE AFFECTS

NURSING ASSESSMENT

CONTRAINDICTIONS

NOTES

CONSIDERATIONS

Pharmacology

GENERIC NAME

BRAND NAME

DRUG CLASS

ROUTE

HIGH ALERT

☐ YES   ☐ NO

THERAPEUTIC USES

MECHANISMS OF ACTION

ADVERSE AFFECTS

NURSING ASSESSMENT

CONTRAINDICTIONS

NOTES

CONSIDERATIONS

Pharmacology

GENERIC NAME

BRAND NAME

DRUG CLASS

ROUTE

HIGH ALERT

☐ YES   ☐ NO

THERAPEUTIC USES

MECHANISMS OF ACTION

ADVERSE AFFECTS

NURSING ASSESSMENT

CONTRAINDICTIONS

NOTES

CONSIDERATIONS

Pharmacology

GENERIC NAME

BRAND NAME

DRUG CLASS

ROUTE

HIGH ALERT

☐ YES   ☐ NO

THERAPEUTIC USES

MECHANISMS OF ACTION

ADVERSE AFFECTS

NURSING ASSESSMENT

CONTRAINDICTIONS

NOTES

CONSIDERATIONS

Pharmacology

GENERIC NAME

BRAND NAME

DRUG CLASS

ROUTE

HIGH ALERT

☐ YES ☐ NO

THERAPEUTIC USES

MECHANISMS OF ACTION

ADVERSE AFFECTS

NURSING ASSESSMENT

CONTRAINDICTIONS

NOTES

CONSIDERATIONS

Pharmacology

GENERIC NAME

BRAND NAME

DRUG CLASS

ROUTE

HIGH ALERT

☐ YES   ☐ NO

THERAPEUTIC USES

MECHANISMS OF ACTION

ADVERSE AFFECTS

NURSING ASSESSMENT

CONTRAINDICTIONS

NOTES

CONSIDERATIONS

Pharmacology

GENERIC NAME

BRAND NAME

DRUG CLASS

ROUTE

HIGH ALERT

☐ YES   ☐ NO

THERAPEUTIC USES

MECHANISMS OF ACTION

ADVERSE AFFECTS

NURSING ASSESSMENT

CONTRAINDICTIONS

NOTES

CONSIDERATIONS

Pharmacology

GENERIC NAME

BRAND NAME

DRUG CLASS

ROUTE

HIGH ALERT

☐ YES   ☐ NO

THERAPEUTIC USES

MECHANISMS OF ACTION

ADVERSE AFFECTS

NURSING ASSESSMENT

CONTRAINDICTIONS

NOTES

CONSIDERATIONS

Pharmacology

GENERIC NAME

BRAND NAME

DRUG CLASS

ROUTE

HIGH ALERT

☐ YES   ☐ NO

THERAPEUTIC USES

MECHANISMS OF ACTION

ADVERSE AFFECTS

NURSING ASSESSMENT

CONTRAINDICTIONS

NOTES

CONSIDERATIONS

Pharmacology

GENERIC NAME

BRAND NAME

DRUG CLASS

ROUTE

HIGH ALERT

☐ YES   ☐ NO

THERAPEUTIC USES

MECHANISMS OF ACTION

ADVERSE AFFECTS

NURSING ASSESSMENT

CONTRAINDICTIONS

CONSIDERATIONS

NOTES

Pharmacology

GENERIC NAME

BRAND NAME

DRUG CLASS

ROUTE

HIGH ALERT

☐ YES ☐ NO

THERAPEUTIC USES

MECHANISMS OF ACTION

ADVERSE AFFECTS

NURSING ASSESSMENT

CONTRAINDICTIONS

NOTES

CONSIDERATIONS

Pharmacology

GENERIC NAME

BRAND NAME

DRUG CLASS

ROUTE

HIGH ALERT

☐ YES   ☐ NO

THERAPEUTIC USES

MECHANISMS OF ACTION

ADVERSE AFFECTS

NURSING ASSESSMENT

CONTRAINDICTIONS

NOTES

CONSIDERATIONS

Pharmacology

GENERIC NAME

BRAND NAME

DRUG CLASS

ROUTE

HIGH ALERT

☐ YES   ☐ NO

THERAPEUTIC USES

MECHANISMS OF ACTION

ADVERSE AFFECTS

NURSING ASSESSMENT

CONTRAINDICTIONS

CONSIDERATIONS

NOTES

Pharmacology

GENERIC NAME

BRAND NAME

DRUG CLASS

ROUTE

HIGH ALERT

☐ YES   ☐ NO

THERAPEUTIC USES

MECHANISMS OF ACTION

ADVERSE AFFECTS

NURSING ASSESSMENT

CONTRAINDICTIONS

NOTES

CONSIDERATIONS

Pharmacology

GENERIC NAME

BRAND NAME

DRUG CLASS

ROUTE

HIGH ALERT

☐ YES   ☐ NO

THERAPEUTIC USES

MECHANISMS OF ACTION

ADVERSE AFFECTS

NURSING ASSESSMENT

CONTRAINDICTIONS

NOTES

CONSIDERATIONS

Pharmacology

GENERIC NAME

BRAND NAME

DRUG CLASS

ROUTE

HIGH ALERT

☐ YES   ☐ NO

THERAPEUTIC USES

MECHANISMS OF ACTION

ADVERSE AFFECTS

NURSING ASSESSMENT

CONTRAINDICTIONS

NOTES

CONSIDERATIONS

Pharmacology

GENERIC NAME

BRAND NAME

DRUG CLASS

ROUTE

HIGH ALERT

☐ YES ☐ NO

THERAPEUTIC USES

MECHANISMS OF ACTION

ADVERSE AFFECTS

NURSING ASSESSMENT

CONTRAINDICTIONS

NOTES

CONSIDERATIONS

Pharmacology

GENERIC NAME

BRAND NAME

DRUG CLASS

ROUTE

HIGH ALERT

☐ YES   ☐ NO

THERAPEUTIC USES

MECHANISMS OF ACTION

ADVERSE AFFECTS

NURSING ASSESSMENT

CONTRAINDICTIONS

NOTES

CONSIDERATIONS

Pharmacology

GENERIC NAME

BRAND NAME

DRUG CLASS

ROUTE

HIGH ALERT

☐ YES ☐ NO

THERAPEUTIC USES

MECHANISMS OF ACTION

ADVERSE AFFECTS

NURSING ASSESSMENT

CONTRAINDICTIONS

NOTES

CONSIDERATIONS

Pharmacology

GENERIC NAME

BRAND NAME

DRUG CLASS

ROUTE

HIGH ALERT

☐ YES   ☐ NO

THERAPEUTIC USES

MECHANISMS OF ACTION

ADVERSE AFFECTS

NURSING ASSESSMENT

CONTRAINDICTIONS

NOTES

CONSIDERATIONS

Pharmacology

GENERIC NAME

BRAND NAME

DRUG CLASS

ROUTE

HIGH ALERT

☐ YES   ☐ NO

THERAPEUTIC USES

MECHANISMS OF ACTION

ADVERSE AFFECTS

NURSING ASSESSMENT

CONTRAINDICTIONS

NOTES

CONSIDERATIONS

Pharmacology

GENERIC NAME

BRAND NAME

DRUG CLASS

ROUTE

HIGH ALERT

☐ YES   ☐ NO

THERAPEUTIC USES

MECHANISMS OF ACTION

ADVERSE AFFECTS

NURSING ASSESSMENT

CONTRAINDICTIONS

NOTES

CONSIDERATIONS

Pharmacology

GENERIC NAME

BRAND NAME

DRUG CLASS

ROUTE

HIGH ALERT

☐ YES   ☐ NO

THERAPEUTIC USES

MECHANISMS OF ACTION

ADVERSE AFFECTS

NURSING ASSESSMENT

CONTRAINDICTIONS

NOTES

CONSIDERATIONS

Pharmacology

GENERIC NAME

BRAND NAME

DRUG CLASS

ROUTE

HIGH ALERT

☐ YES ☐ NO

THERAPEUTIC USES

MECHANISMS OF ACTION

ADVERSE AFFECTS

NURSING ASSESSMENT

CONTRAINDICTIONS

NOTES

CONSIDERATIONS

Pharmacology

GENERIC NAME

BRAND NAME

DRUG CLASS

ROUTE

HIGH ALERT

☐ YES ☐ NO

THERAPEUTIC USES

MECHANISMS OF ACTION

ADVERSE AFFECTS

NURSING ASSESSMENT

CONTRAINDICTIONS

NOTES

CONSIDERATIONS

Pharmacology

GENERIC NAME

BRAND NAME

DRUG CLASS

ROUTE

HIGH ALERT

☐ YES   ☐ NO

THERAPEUTIC USES

MECHANISMS OF ACTION

ADVERSE AFFECTS

NURSING ASSESSMENT

CONTRAINDICTIONS

NOTES

CONSIDERATIONS

Pharmacology

GENERIC NAME

BRAND NAME

DRUG CLASS

ROUTE

HIGH ALERT

☐ YES   ☐ NO

THERAPEUTIC USES

MECHANISMS OF ACTION

ADVERSE AFFECTS

NURSING ASSESSMENT

CONTRAINDICTIONS

NOTES

CONSIDERATIONS

Pharmacology

GENERIC NAME

BRAND NAME

DRUG CLASS

ROUTE

HIGH ALERT

☐ YES ☐ NO

THERAPEUTIC USES

MECHANISMS OF ACTION

ADVERSE AFFECTS

NURSING ASSESSMENT

CONTRAINDICTIONS

NOTES

CONSIDERATIONS

Pharmacology

GENERIC NAME

BRAND NAME

DRUG CLASS

ROUTE

HIGH ALERT

☐ YES   ☐ NO

THERAPEUTIC USES

MECHANISMS OF ACTION

ADVERSE AFFECTS

NURSING ASSESSMENT

CONTRAINDICTIONS

NOTES

CONSIDERATIONS

Pharmacology

GENERIC NAME

BRAND NAME

DRUG CLASS

ROUTE

HIGH ALERT

☐ YES ☐ NO

THERAPEUTIC USES

MECHANISMS OF ACTION

ADVERSE AFFECTS

NURSING ASSESSMENT

CONTRAINDICTIONS

NOTES

CONSIDERATIONS

Pharmacology

GENERIC NAME

BRAND NAME

DRUG CLASS

ROUTE

HIGH ALERT

☐ YES ☐ NO

THERAPEUTIC USES

MECHANISMS OF ACTION

ADVERSE AFFECTS

NURSING ASSESSMENT

CONTRAINDICTIONS

NOTES

CONSIDERATIONS

Pharmacology

GENERIC NAME

BRAND NAME

DRUG CLASS

ROUTE

HIGH ALERT

☐ YES   ☐ NO

THERAPEUTIC USES

MECHANISMS OF ACTION

ADVERSE AFFECTS

NURSING ASSESSMENT

CONTRAINDICTIONS

NOTES

CONSIDERATIONS

Pharmacology

GENERIC NAME

BRAND NAME

DRUG CLASS

ROUTE

HIGH ALERT

☐ YES   ☐ NO

THERAPEUTIC USES

MECHANISMS OF ACTION

ADVERSE AFFECTS

NURSING ASSESSMENT

CONTRAINDICTIONS

NOTES

CONSIDERATIONS

Pharmacology

GENERIC NAME

BRAND NAME

DRUG CLASS

ROUTE

HIGH ALERT

☐ YES   ☐ NO

THERAPEUTIC USES

MECHANISMS OF ACTION

ADVERSE AFFECTS

NURSING ASSESSMENT

CONTRAINDICTIONS

NOTES

CONSIDERATIONS

Pharmacology

GENERIC NAME

BRAND NAME

DRUG CLASS

ROUTE

HIGH ALERT

☐ YES　　☐ NO

THERAPEUTIC USES

MECHANISMS OF ACTION

ADVERSE AFFECTS

NURSING ASSESSMENT

CONTRAINDICTIONS

NOTES

CONSIDERATIONS

Pharmacology

GENERIC NAME

BRAND NAME

DRUG CLASS

ROUTE

HIGH ALERT

☐ YES　　☐ NO

THERAPEUTIC USES

MECHANISMS OF ACTION

ADVERSE AFFECTS

NURSING ASSESSMENT

CONTRAINDICTIONS

NOTES

CONSIDERATIONS

Pharmacology

GENERIC NAME

BRAND NAME

DRUG CLASS

ROUTE

HIGH ALERT

☐ YES   ☐ NO

THERAPEUTIC USES

MECHANISMS OF ACTION

ADVERSE AFFECTS

NURSING ASSESSMENT

CONTRAINDICTIONS

NOTES

CONSIDERATIONS

Pharmacology

GENERIC NAME

BRAND NAME

DRUG CLASS

ROUTE

HIGH ALERT

☐ YES   ☐ NO

THERAPEUTIC USES

MECHANISMS OF ACTION

ADVERSE AFFECTS

NURSING ASSESSMENT

CONTRAINDICTIONS

NOTES

CONSIDERATIONS

Pharmacology

GENERIC NAME

BRAND NAME

DRUG CLASS

ROUTE

HIGH ALERT

☐ YES ☐ NO

THERAPEUTIC USES

MECHANISMS OF ACTION

ADVERSE AFFECTS

NURSING ASSESSMENT

CONTRAINDICTIONS

NOTES

CONSIDERATIONS

Pharmacology

GENERIC NAME

BRAND NAME

DRUG CLASS

ROUTE

HIGH ALERT

☐ YES   ☐ NO

THERAPEUTIC USES

MECHANISMS OF ACTION

ADVERSE AFFECTS

NURSING ASSESSMENT

CONTRAINDICTIONS

NOTES

CONSIDERATIONS

Pharmacology

GENERIC NAME

BRAND NAME

DRUG CLASS

ROUTE

HIGH ALERT

☐ YES   ☐ NO

THERAPEUTIC USES

MECHANISMS OF ACTION

ADVERSE AFFECTS

NURSING ASSESSMENT

CONTRAINDICTIONS

NOTES

CONSIDERATIONS

Pharmacology

GENERIC NAME

BRAND NAME

DRUG CLASS

ROUTE

HIGH ALERT

☐ YES   ☐ NO

THERAPEUTIC USES

MECHANISMS OF ACTION

ADVERSE AFFECTS

NURSING ASSESSMENT

CONTRAINDICTIONS

NOTES

CONSIDERATIONS

Pharmacology

GENERIC NAME

BRAND NAME

DRUG CLASS

ROUTE

HIGH ALERT

☐ YES ☐ NO

THERAPEUTIC USES

MECHANISMS OF ACTION

ADVERSE AFFECTS

NURSING ASSESSMENT

CONTRAINDICTIONS

NOTES

CONSIDERATIONS

Pharmacology

GENERIC NAME

BRAND NAME

DRUG CLASS

ROUTE

HIGH ALERT

☐ YES ☐ NO

THERAPEUTIC USES

MECHANISMS OF ACTION

ADVERSE AFFECTS

NURSING ASSESSMENT

CONTRAINDICTIONS

NOTES

CONSIDERATIONS

Pharmacology

GENERIC NAME

BRAND NAME

DRUG CLASS

ROUTE

HIGH ALERT

☐ YES ☐ NO

THERAPEUTIC USES

MECHANISMS OF ACTION

ADVERSE AFFECTS

NURSING ASSESSMENT

CONTRAINDICTIONS

NOTES

CONSIDERATIONS

Pharmacology

GENERIC NAME

BRAND NAME

DRUG CLASS

ROUTE

HIGH ALERT

☐ YES   ☐ NO

THERAPEUTIC USES

MECHANISMS OF ACTION

ADVERSE AFFECTS

NURSING ASSESSMENT

CONTRAINDICTIONS

NOTES

CONSIDERATIONS

Pharmacology

GENERIC NAME

BRAND NAME

DRUG CLASS

ROUTE

HIGH ALERT

☐ YES   ☐ NO

THERAPEUTIC USES

MECHANISMS OF ACTION

ADVERSE AFFECTS

NURSING ASSESSMENT

CONTRAINDICTIONS

NOTES

CONSIDERATIONS

Pharmacology

GENERIC NAME

BRAND NAME

DRUG CLASS

ROUTE

HIGH ALERT

☐ YES ☐ NO

THERAPEUTIC USES

MECHANISMS OF ACTION

ADVERSE AFFECTS

NURSING ASSESSMENT

CONTRAINDICTIONS

NOTES

CONSIDERATIONS

Pharmacology

GENERIC NAME

BRAND NAME

DRUG CLASS

ROUTE

HIGH ALERT

☐ YES   ☐ NO

THERAPEUTIC USES

MECHANISMS OF ACTION

ADVERSE AFFECTS

NURSING ASSESSMENT

CONTRAINDICTIONS

NOTES

CONSIDERATIONS

Pharmacology

GENERIC NAME

BRAND NAME

DRUG CLASS

ROUTE

HIGH ALERT

☐ YES ☐ NO

THERAPEUTIC USES

MECHANISMS OF ACTION

ADVERSE AFFECTS

NURSING ASSESSMENT

CONTRAINDICTIONS

NOTES

CONSIDERATIONS

Pharmacology

GENERIC NAME

BRAND NAME

DRUG CLASS

ROUTE

HIGH ALERT

☐ YES ☐ NO

THERAPEUTIC USES

MECHANISMS OF ACTION

ADVERSE AFFECTS

NURSING ASSESSMENT

CONTRAINDICTIONS

NOTES

CONSIDERATIONS

Pharmacology

GENERIC NAME

BRAND NAME

DRUG CLASS

ROUTE

HIGH ALERT

☐ YES   ☐ NO

THERAPEUTIC USES

MECHANISMS OF ACTION

ADVERSE AFFECTS

NURSING ASSESSMENT

CONTRAINDICTIONS

NOTES

CONSIDERATIONS

Pharmacology

GENERIC NAME

BRAND NAME

DRUG CLASS

ROUTE

HIGH ALERT

☐ YES   ☐ NO

THERAPEUTIC USES

MECHANISMS OF ACTION

ADVERSE AFFECTS

NURSING ASSESSMENT

CONTRAINDICTIONS

CONSIDERATIONS

NOTES

Pharmacology

GENERIC NAME

BRAND NAME

DRUG CLASS

ROUTE

HIGH ALERT

☐ YES　　☐ NO

THERAPEUTIC USES

MECHANISMS OF ACTION

ADVERSE AFFECTS

NURSING ASSESSMENT

CONTRAINDICTIONS

NOTES

CONSIDERATIONS

Pharmacology

GENERIC NAME

BRAND NAME

DRUG CLASS

ROUTE

HIGH ALERT

☐ YES ☐ NO

THERAPEUTIC USES

MECHANISMS OF ACTION

ADVERSE AFFECTS

NURSING ASSESSMENT

CONTRAINDICTIONS

NOTES

CONSIDERATIONS

Pharmacology

GENERIC NAME

BRAND NAME

DRUG CLASS

ROUTE

HIGH ALERT

☐ YES   ☐ NO

THERAPEUTIC USES

MECHANISMS OF ACTION

ADVERSE AFFECTS

NURSING ASSESSMENT

CONTRAINDICTIONS

NOTES

CONSIDERATIONS

Pharmacology

GENERIC NAME

BRAND NAME

DRUG CLASS

ROUTE

HIGH ALERT

☐ YES ☐ NO

THERAPEUTIC USES

MECHANISMS OF ACTION

ADVERSE AFFECTS

NURSING ASSESSMENT

CONTRAINDICTIONS

NOTES

CONSIDERATIONS

Pharmacology

GENERIC NAME

BRAND NAME

DRUG CLASS

ROUTE

HIGH ALERT

☐ YES   ☐ NO

THERAPEUTIC USES

MECHANISMS OF ACTION

ADVERSE AFFECTS

NURSING ASSESSMENT

CONTRAINDICTIONS

NOTES

CONSIDERATIONS

Pharmacology

GENERIC NAME

BRAND NAME

DRUG CLASS

ROUTE

HIGH ALERT

☐ YES   ☐ NO

THERAPEUTIC USES

MECHANISMS OF ACTION

ADVERSE AFFECTS

NURSING ASSESSMENT

CONTRAINDICTIONS

NOTES

CONSIDERATIONS

Pharmacology

GENERIC NAME

BRAND NAME

DRUG CLASS

ROUTE

HIGH ALERT

☐ YES ☐ NO

THERAPEUTIC USES

MECHANISMS OF ACTION

ADVERSE AFFECTS

NURSING ASSESSMENT

CONTRAINDICTIONS

CONSIDERATIONS

NOTES

Pharmacology

GENERIC NAME

BRAND NAME

DRUG CLASS

ROUTE

HIGH ALERT

☐ YES ☐ NO

THERAPEUTIC USES

MECHANISMS OF ACTION

ADVERSE AFFECTS

NURSING ASSESSMENT

CONTRAINDICTIONS

NOTES

CONSIDERATIONS

Pharmacology

GENERIC NAME

BRAND NAME

DRUG CLASS

ROUTE

HIGH ALERT

☐ YES   ☐ NO

THERAPEUTIC USES

MECHANISMS OF ACTION

ADVERSE AFFECTS

NURSING ASSESSMENT

CONTRAINDICTIONS

NOTES

CONSIDERATIONS

Pharmacology

GENERIC NAME

BRAND NAME

DRUG CLASS

ROUTE

HIGH ALERT

☐ YES   ☐ NO

THERAPEUTIC USES

MECHANISMS OF ACTION

ADVERSE AFFECTS

NURSING ASSESSMENT

CONTRAINDICTIONS

NOTES

CONSIDERATIONS

Pharmacology

GENERIC NAME

BRAND NAME

DRUG CLASS

ROUTE

HIGH ALERT

☐ YES ☐ NO

THERAPEUTIC USES

MECHANISMS OF ACTION

ADVERSE AFFECTS

NURSING ASSESSMENT

CONTRAINDICTIONS

NOTES

CONSIDERATIONS

Pharmacology

GENERIC NAME

BRAND NAME

DRUG CLASS

ROUTE

HIGH ALERT

☐ YES ☐ NO

THERAPEUTIC USES

MECHANISMS OF ACTION

ADVERSE AFFECTS

NURSING ASSESSMENT

CONTRAINDICTIONS

CONSIDERATIONS

NOTES

Pharmacology

GENERIC NAME

BRAND NAME

DRUG CLASS

ROUTE

HIGH ALERT

☐ YES ☐ NO

THERAPEUTIC USES

MECHANISMS OF ACTION

ADVERSE AFFECTS

NURSING ASSESSMENT

CONTRAINDICTIONS

CONSIDERATIONS

NOTES

Pharmacology

GENERIC NAME

BRAND NAME

DRUG CLASS

ROUTE

HIGH ALERT

☐ YES ☐ NO

THERAPEUTIC USES

MECHANISMS OF ACTION

ADVERSE AFFECTS

NURSING ASSESSMENT

CONTRAINDICTIONS

NOTES

CONSIDERATIONS

Pharmacology

GENERIC NAME

BRAND NAME

DRUG CLASS

ROUTE

HIGH ALERT

☐ YES   ☐ NO

THERAPEUTIC USES

MECHANISMS OF ACTION

ADVERSE AFFECTS

NURSING ASSESSMENT

CONTRAINDICTIONS

NOTES

CONSIDERATIONS

Pharmacology

GENERIC NAME

BRAND NAME

DRUG CLASS

ROUTE

HIGH ALERT

☐ YES   ☐ NO

THERAPEUTIC USES

MECHANISMS OF ACTION

ADVERSE AFFECTS

NURSING ASSESSMENT

CONTRAINDICTIONS

CONSIDERATIONS

NOTES

Pharmacology

GENERIC NAME

BRAND NAME

DRUG CLASS

ROUTE

HIGH ALERT

☐ YES   ☐ NO

THERAPEUTIC USES

MECHANISMS OF ACTION

ADVERSE AFFECTS

NURSING ASSESSMENT

CONTRAINDICTIONS

NOTES

CONSIDERATIONS

Pharmacology

GENERIC NAME

BRAND NAME

DRUG CLASS

ROUTE

HIGH ALERT

☐ YES   ☐ NO

THERAPEUTIC USES

MECHANISMS OF ACTION

ADVERSE AFFECTS

NURSING ASSESSMENT

CONTRAINDICTIONS

NOTES

CONSIDERATIONS

Pharmacology

GENERIC NAME

BRAND NAME

DRUG CLASS

ROUTE

HIGH ALERT

☐ YES   ☐ NO

THERAPEUTIC USES

MECHANISMS OF ACTION

ADVERSE AFFECTS

NURSING ASSESSMENT

CONTRAINDICTIONS

NOTES

CONSIDERATIONS

Pharmacology

GENERIC NAME

BRAND NAME

DRUG CLASS

ROUTE

HIGH ALERT

☐ YES   ☐ NO

THERAPEUTIC USES

MECHANISMS OF ACTION

ADVERSE AFFECTS

NURSING ASSESSMENT

CONTRAINDICTIONS

NOTES

CONSIDERATIONS

Pharmacology

GENERIC NAME

BRAND NAME

DRUG CLASS

ROUTE

HIGH ALERT

☐ YES   ☐ NO

THERAPEUTIC USES

MECHANISMS OF ACTION

ADVERSE AFFECTS

NURSING ASSESSMENT

CONTRAINDICTIONS

CONSIDERATIONS

NOTES

Pharmacology

GENERIC NAME

BRAND NAME

DRUG CLASS

ROUTE

HIGH ALERT

☐ YES   ☐ NO

THERAPEUTIC USES

MECHANISMS OF ACTION

ADVERSE AFFECTS

NURSING ASSESSMENT

CONTRAINDICTIONS

NOTES

CONSIDERATIONS

Pharmacology

GENERIC NAME

BRAND NAME

DRUG CLASS

ROUTE

HIGH ALERT

☐ YES　　☐ NO

THERAPEUTIC USES

MECHANISMS OF ACTION

ADVERSE AFFECTS

NURSING ASSESSMENT

CONTRAINDICTIONS

NOTES

CONSIDERATIONS

Pharmacology

GENERIC NAME

BRAND NAME

DRUG CLASS

ROUTE

HIGH ALERT

☐ YES ☐ NO

THERAPEUTIC USES

MECHANISMS OF ACTION

ADVERSE AFFECTS

NURSING ASSESSMENT

CONTRAINDICTIONS

NOTES

CONSIDERATIONS

Pharmacology

GENERIC NAME

BRAND NAME

DRUG CLASS

ROUTE

HIGH ALERT

☐ YES   ☐ NO

THERAPEUTIC USES

MECHANISMS OF ACTION

ADVERSE AFFECTS

NURSING ASSESSMENT

CONTRAINDICTIONS

CONSIDERATIONS

NOTES

Pharmacology

GENERIC NAME

BRAND NAME

DRUG CLASS

ROUTE

HIGH ALERT

☐ YES   ☐ NO

THERAPEUTIC USES

MECHANISMS OF ACTION

ADVERSE AFFECTS

NURSING ASSESSMENT

CONTRAINDICTIONS

NOTES

CONSIDERATIONS

Pharmacology

GENERIC NAME

BRAND NAME

DRUG CLASS

ROUTE

HIGH ALERT

☐ YES   ☐ NO

THERAPEUTIC USES

MECHANISMS OF ACTION

ADVERSE AFFECTS

NURSING ASSESSMENT

CONTRAINDICTIONS

NOTES

CONSIDERATIONS

Pharmacology

GENERIC NAME

BRAND NAME

DRUG CLASS

ROUTE

HIGH ALERT

☐ YES   ☐ NO

THERAPEUTIC USES

MECHANISMS OF ACTION

ADVERSE AFFECTS

NURSING ASSESSMENT

CONTRAINDICTIONS

NOTES

CONSIDERATIONS

Pharmacology

GENERIC NAME

BRAND NAME

DRUG CLASS

ROUTE

HIGH ALERT

☐ YES   ☐ NO

THERAPEUTIC USES

MECHANISMS OF ACTION

ADVERSE AFFECTS

NURSING ASSESSMENT

CONTRAINDICTIONS

CONSIDERATIONS

NOTES

Pharmacology

GENERIC NAME

BRAND NAME

DRUG CLASS

ROUTE

HIGH ALERT

☐ YES ☐ NO

THERAPEUTIC USES

MECHANISMS OF ACTION

ADVERSE AFFECTS

NURSING ASSESSMENT

CONTRAINDICTIONS

NOTES

CONSIDERATIONS

Pharmacology

GENERIC NAME

BRAND NAME

DRUG CLASS

ROUTE

HIGH ALERT

☐ YES   ☐ NO

THERAPEUTIC USES

MECHANISMS OF ACTION

ADVERSE AFFECTS

NURSING ASSESSMENT

CONTRAINDICTIONS

NOTES

CONSIDERATIONS

Pharmacology

GENERIC NAME

BRAND NAME

DRUG CLASS

ROUTE

HIGH ALERT

☐ YES   ☐ NO

THERAPEUTIC USES

MECHANISMS OF ACTION

ADVERSE AFFECTS

NURSING ASSESSMENT

CONTRAINDICTIONS

NOTES

CONSIDERATIONS

Pharmacology

GENERIC NAME _____   BRAND NAME _____

DRUG CLASS

ROUTE

HIGH ALERT

☐ YES   ☐ NO

THERAPEUTIC USES

MECHANISMS OF ACTION

ADVERSE AFFECTS

NURSING ASSESSMENT

CONTRAINDICTIONS

CONSIDERATIONS

NOTES

Pharmacology

GENERIC NAME

BRAND NAME

DRUG CLASS

ROUTE

HIGH ALERT

☐ YES   ☐ NO

THERAPEUTIC USES

MECHANISMS OF ACTION

ADVERSE AFFECTS

NURSING ASSESSMENT

CONTRAINDICTIONS

NOTES

CONSIDERATIONS

Pharmacology

GENERIC NAME

BRAND NAME

DRUG CLASS

ROUTE

HIGH ALERT

☐ YES ☐ NO

THERAPEUTIC USES

MECHANISMS OF ACTION

ADVERSE AFFECTS

NURSING ASSESSMENT

CONTRAINDICTIONS

NOTES

CONSIDERATIONS

Pharmacology

GENERIC NAME

BRAND NAME

DRUG CLASS

ROUTE

HIGH ALERT

☐ YES   ☐ NO

THERAPEUTIC USES

MECHANISMS OF ACTION

ADVERSE AFFECTS

NURSING ASSESSMENT

CONTRAINDICTIONS

NOTES

CONSIDERATIONS

Pharmacology

GENERIC NAME

BRAND NAME

DRUG CLASS

ROUTE

HIGH ALERT

☐ YES   ☐ NO

THERAPEUTIC USES

MECHANISMS OF ACTION

ADVERSE AFFECTS

NURSING ASSESSMENT

CONTRAINDICTIONS

NOTES

CONSIDERATIONS

Pharmacology

GENERIC NAME

BRAND NAME

DRUG CLASS

ROUTE

HIGH ALERT

☐ YES ☐ NO

THERAPEUTIC USES

MECHANISMS OF ACTION

ADVERSE AFFECTS

NURSING ASSESSMENT

CONTRAINDICTIONS

NOTES

CONSIDERATIONS

Pharmacology

GENERIC NAME

BRAND NAME

DRUG CLASS

ROUTE

HIGH ALERT

☐ YES   ☐ NO

THERAPEUTIC USES

MECHANISMS OF ACTION

ADVERSE AFFECTS

NURSING ASSESSMENT

CONTRAINDICTIONS

NOTES

CONSIDERATIONS

Pharmacology

GENERIC NAME

BRAND NAME

DRUG CLASS

ROUTE

HIGH ALERT

☐ YES   ☐ NO

THERAPEUTIC USES

MECHANISMS OF ACTION

ADVERSE AFFECTS

NURSING ASSESSMENT

CONTRAINDICTIONS

CONSIDERATIONS

NOTES

Pharmacology

GENERIC NAME

BRAND NAME

DRUG CLASS

ROUTE

HIGH ALERT

☐ YES   ☐ NO

THERAPEUTIC USES

MECHANISMS OF ACTION

ADVERSE AFFECTS

NURSING ASSESSMENT

CONTRAINDICTIONS

NOTES

CONSIDERATIONS

Pharmacology

GENERIC NAME

BRAND NAME

DRUG CLASS

ROUTE

HIGH ALERT

☐ YES   ☐ NO

THERAPEUTIC USES

MECHANISMS OF ACTION

ADVERSE AFFECTS

NURSING ASSESSMENT

CONTRAINDICTIONS

NOTES

CONSIDERATIONS

Pharmacology

GENERIC NAME

BRAND NAME

DRUG CLASS

ROUTE

HIGH ALERT

☐ YES ☐ NO

THERAPEUTIC USES

MECHANISMS OF ACTION

ADVERSE AFFECTS

NURSING ASSESSMENT

CONTRAINDICTIONS

NOTES

CONSIDERATIONS

Pharmacology

GENERIC NAME

BRAND NAME

DRUG CLASS

ROUTE

HIGH ALERT

☐ YES   ☐ NO

THERAPEUTIC USES

MECHANISMS OF ACTION

ADVERSE AFFECTS

NURSING ASSESSMENT

CONTRAINDICTIONS

NOTES

CONSIDERATIONS

Pharmacology

GENERIC NAME

BRAND NAME

DRUG CLASS

ROUTE

HIGH ALERT

☐ YES   ☐ NO

THERAPEUTIC USES

MECHANISMS OF ACTION

ADVERSE AFFECTS

NURSING ASSESSMENT

CONTRAINDICTIONS

CONSIDERATIONS

NOTES

Pharmacology

GENERIC NAME

BRAND NAME

DRUG CLASS

ROUTE

HIGH ALERT

☐ YES ☐ NO

THERAPEUTIC USES

MECHANISMS OF ACTION

ADVERSE AFFECTS

NURSING ASSESSMENT

CONTRAINDICTIONS

NOTES

CONSIDERATIONS

Pharmacology

GENERIC NAME

BRAND NAME

DRUG CLASS

ROUTE

HIGH ALERT

☐ YES   ☐ NO

THERAPEUTIC USES

MECHANISMS OF ACTION

ADVERSE AFFECTS

NURSING ASSESSMENT

CONTRAINDICTIONS

NOTES

CONSIDERATIONS

Pharmacology

GENERIC NAME

BRAND NAME

DRUG CLASS

ROUTE

HIGH ALERT

☐ YES   ☐ NO

THERAPEUTIC USES

MECHANISMS OF ACTION

ADVERSE AFFECTS

NURSING ASSESSMENT

CONTRAINDICTIONS

NOTES

CONSIDERATIONS

Pharmacology

GENERIC NAME

BRAND NAME

DRUG CLASS

ROUTE

HIGH ALERT

☐ YES   ☐ NO

THERAPEUTIC USES

MECHANISMS OF ACTION

ADVERSE AFFECTS

NURSING ASSESSMENT

CONTRAINDICTIONS

NOTES

CONSIDERATIONS

Made in the USA
Monee, IL
02 December 2022

19406980R00059